A Word Mastery Series

Essential Words

Activity Book

Math

NEW LEAF

EDUCATION

New Leaf Education

www.newleafeducation.com

Visit us on the web at www.newleafeducation.com to learn more about our products.

Design and Cover Illustration:
Sasha Blanton

Printed in the United States of America

ISBN: 1-933655-04-6

10 9 8 7 6 5 4 3 2 1

Contents

Welcome!

Math
Activity Book!

About this book:

In this book, you will find activities to help you learn each term in the Math Glossary. There are nearly 220 words to practice while learning and having fun!

Activity Sheets include:

Word Bar with the terms

Different kinds of activities to help with understanding

Page numbers to help you find terms in the Glossary

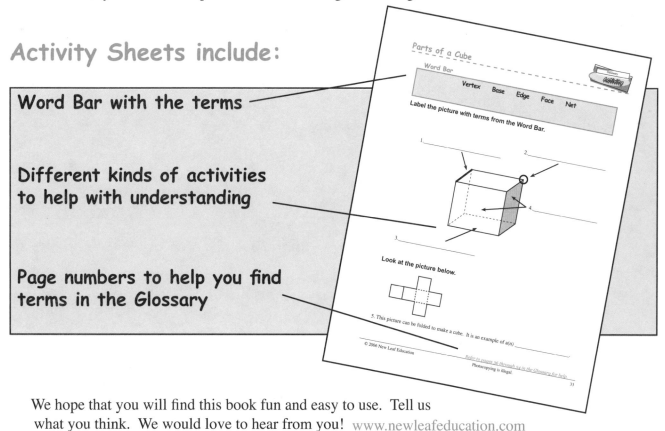

We hope that you will find this book fun and easy to use. Tell us what you think. We would love to hear from you! www.newleafeducation.com

Add and Subtract

Word Bar

| Add | Addend | Fact family | Subtract | Difference | Sum |

Compatible numbers

Label the pictures using terms from the Word Bar.

$$7 + 2 = 9$$

1. When you _____ 7 and 2, you get 9.

2. 7 and 2 are called the _____ s.

3. 9 is the _____ .

$$9 - 2 = 7$$

4. When you _____ 2 from 9, you get 7.

5. 7 is the _____ of 9 and 2.

7 + 2 = 9	9 – 2 = 7
2 + 7 = 9	9 – 7 = 2

6. 2, 7, and 9 make up this _____ .

7. It is easier to add 10 and 20 than 11 and 19. 10 and 20 are

_____ .

Refer to pages 1 through 23 in the Glossary for help.

Word Bar

Integers	Whole numbers	Odd number	Even number

Fill in the blanks with terms from the Word Bar.

1. A number that can be divided evenly by 2 is called a(n) _____.

2. A number that cannot be divided evenly by 2 is called a(n)_____.

3. Circle the even numbers. Cross out the odd numbers.

4   77   2   7   15   8   92   6   29   5

4. {0, 1, 2, 3, 4...} shows the set of _____.

5. { ...-3, -2, -1, 0, 1, 2, 3...} shows the set of _____.

Refer to pages 9 through 25 in the Glossary for help.

© 2006 New Leaf Education   Photocopying is illegal.

Place Value

Word Bar

Tens place	Hundreds place	Thousands place
Place value	Digit	Standard form
Expanded notation	Millions place	

Look at the number. Then answer the questions.

2,478,935

1. The 2, the 4, and the 7 are examples of _____s. They are all number symbols.

2. The 2 is in the _____ place.

3. The 3 is in the _____ place.

4. The 8 is in the _____ place.

5. The 9 is in the _____ place.

6. The _____ for the digit 5 is the ones place.

7. Write 13,416 in **expanded notation**.

8. Write 6,000 + 400 + 8 in **standard form**.

Refer to pages 6 through 24 in the Glossary for help.

Word Bar

Greater than sign Inequality	Less than sign	Equal

Label each symbol.

1. **<** _____

2. **>** _____

Fill in the sentences.

3. 9 is (**greater** less) than 4. It is written like this: 9 _____ 4.

4. 12 is (**greater** less) than 15. It is written like this: 12 _____ 15.

5. 6 is the same as 6. Another way to say this is that 6 _____s 6.

6. When something is not the same amount as another, you use **<** or **>**. An

expression that uses **<** or **>** is called a(n) _____.

Refer to pages 8 through 15 in the Glossary for help.

Estimating

Word Bar

Round	Estimate	Greatest	Least	Number line

Follow the directions.

{6, 8, 3, 9, 6, 2}

1. The number 2 is the _____ in this set. It is the smallest number.

2. The number 9 is the _____ in this set. It is the biggest number.

3. The number 52 _____s to 50.

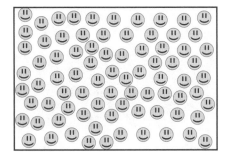

4. **Estimate** how many pictures are in this box. Circle your answer.

10   100   1,000

5. You can use a _____ to help you round.

Refer to pages 9 through 21 in the Glossary for help.

Word Bar

Commutative Property of Addition   Identity Property of Addition
Associative Property of Addition   Distributive Property

Match the example to the correct term.

1. $5 + 4 = 4 + 5$

   a. Associative Property of Addition

2. $8 + 0 = 8$

   b. Commutative Property of Addition

3. $(6 + 3) + 2 = 6 + (3 + 2)$

   c. Distributive Property

4. $6 (4 + 3) = 6 \times 4 + 6 \times 3$

   d. Identity Property of Addition

Give an example of each property.

5. Associative Property of Addition   _____

6. Commutative Property of Addition   _____

7. Distributive Property   _____

8. Identity Property of Addition   _____

Refer to pages 2 through 12 in the Glossary for help.

Multiples and Factors

Word Bar

> **Common factor**   **Common multiple**   **Least common multiple**
> **Greatest common factor**

Follow the directions.

1. The multiples of 3 and 5 are shown below. Circle the **common multiples**.

Multiples of 3: 3, 6, 9, 12, 15, 18, 21, 24, 27, 30

Multiples of 5: 5, 10, 15, 20, 25, 30, 35, 40

2. The multiples of 3 and 4 are shown below. Circle the **least common multiple**.

Multiples of 3: 3, 6, 9, 12, 15, 18, 21, 24, 27

Multiples of 4: 4, 8, 12, 16, 20, 24, 28

3. List the factors of 8 and 12. Circle the **common factors**.

Factors of 8:

Factors of 12:

4. What is the **greatest common factor** of 8 and 12?

Refer to pages 3 through 15 in the Glossary for help.

Word Bar

Multiply   Multiple   Factor   Product   Array

Answer the questions using terms from the Word Bar.

1. This picture shows a 2 by 4 _____. It is arranged in 2 rows and 4 columns.

2. When you _____2 and 4, you get 8.

3. 2 and 4 are _____s of 8. 8 and 1 are also _____s of 8.

4. 8 is a _____of 2 and 4. 16 is also a _____ of 2 and 4.

5. 8 is the result of 2 × 4. The result of multiplication is called a _____.

Refer to pages 1 through 19 in the Glossary for help.

Factoring

Word Bar

Prime factorization	Composite number	Prime number

Look at the diagram. Then answer the questions using terms from the Word Bar.

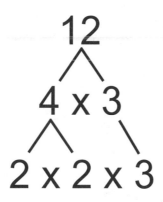

12

4 x 3

2 x 2 x 3

1. 2 and 3 are _____s. They have only 2 factors.

2. 12 is a _____. 12 has more than 2 factors.

3. The picture above shows the _____ of the number 12.

4. Show the **prime factorization** of 15. Circle the **prime numbers**.

Refer to pages 4 through 18 in the Glossary for help.

Word Bar

Commutative Property of Multiplication   Identity Property of Multiplication
Associative Property of Multiplication   Zero Property of Multiplication
Distributive Property

Match the example to the correct term.

1. 5 (2+ 3) = 5 × 2 + 5 × 3   a. Associative Property of Multiplication

2. 8 × 0 = 0   b. Commutative Property of Multiplication

3. 3 × (4 × 5) = (3 × 4) × 5   c. Distributive Property

4. 4 × 1 = 4   d. Identity Property of Multiplication

5. 6 × 4 = 4 × 6   e. Zero Property of Multiplication

Give an example of each property.

6. Associative Property of Multiplication   _____

7. Commutative Property of Multiplication   _____

8. Distributive Property   _____

9. Identity Property of Multiplication   _____

10. Zero Property of Multiplication   _____

Refer to pages 2 through 25 in the Glossary for help.

Word Bar

Divide	Dividend	Divisor	Divisible	Quotient	Remainder

Answer the questions using terms from the Word Bar.

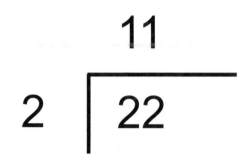

$$2\overline{)22}$$ with quotient 11

1. 2 is the _____.

2. 22 is the _____.

3. 11 is the _____ .

4. 22 is _____ by 2. When 22 is divided by 2, it has no remainder.

5. If you divide 23 by 2, you get 11 R1. The number 1 is the _____ , or the number that is left over.

6. When you _____ a number, you show how many groups or how many in each group.

Refer to pages 7 through 21 in the Glossary for help.

Word Bar

Fraction	Proper fraction	Improper fraction
Numerator	Denominator	Reciprocals
Least common denominator		Mixed numbers

Connect with the correct term on the right.

1. $\dfrac{2}{3}$

a. Denominator

2. $\dfrac{5}{4}$

b. Improper fraction

3. $\dfrac{6}{1}$ and $\dfrac{1}{6}$

c. Least common denominator

4. $3\dfrac{1}{4}$

d. Mixed number

5. $\dfrac{5}{8}$ ←

e. Numerator

6. $\dfrac{5}{8}$ ←

f. Proper fraction

7. for $\dfrac{3}{4}$ and $\dfrac{1}{2}$, this is 8

g. Reciprocals

8. $\dfrac{1}{2}$, $\dfrac{4}{3}$, and $\dfrac{12}{17}$ are examples of _____s. Some are proper while others are improper.

Refer to pages 5 through 20 in the Glossary for help.

© 2006 New Leaf Education

More Fractions

Word Bar

Common denominator	Simplify	Equivalent fractions
Simplest form		

Look at the example. Answer the questions using terms from the Word Bar.

$$\begin{array}{cc} \dfrac{1}{3} & \dfrac{4}{12} \\[2ex] +\dfrac{1}{2} & \dfrac{6}{12} \\[1ex] \hline & \dfrac{10}{12} = \dfrac{5}{6} \end{array}$$

1. The 12 shown above is the _____ for $\frac{1}{2}$ and $\frac{1}{3}$.

2. You can _____ $\frac{10}{12}$ to $\frac{5}{6}$ by dividing the numerator and the

denominator by 2.

3. $\frac{5}{6}$ is in _____ . It cannot be further reduced.

4. $\frac{1}{3}$ and $\frac{4}{12}$ are _____ . They are fractions that have

the same value.

Refer to pages 2 through 22 in the Glossary for help.

Word Bar

Decimal	Decimal point	Equivalent decimals
Repeating decimal	Hundredths place	Tenths place
Thousandths place		

Follow the directions.

1. A number that shows tenths, hundredths, and thousandths is called a _____.

Match the terms with the best choice.

2. Decimal point   a. 1.33333333333…

3. Equivalent decimals   b. 6.547
                              ↑

4. Repeating decimal   c. 72.014
                              ↑

5. Hundredths place   d. 6.5
                              ↑

6. Tenths place   e. 2.115
                              ↑

7. Thousandths place   f. 0.25 and 0.250

Refer to pages 5 through 24 in the Glossary for help.

Rate, Ratio, and Percent

Word Bar

Proportion	Rate	Ratio	Percent	Discount

Look at the picture. Then answer the questions.

Model Car Sale!!!

Regular price: $20.00

Sale: $12.00!

1. The regular price is $20.00. The sale price is $12.00. The _____, or the amount taken off, is $8.00.

2. 4 out of the 8 cars are white. 50_____ of the cars are white.

3. Each car costs $1.50.

"$1.50 per car" is an example of _____, which

compares two quantities measured in different amounts.

4. The _____ of black cars to total cars is 4 to 8.

5. There are 8 cars in 1 set. You can write out a _____ to find the number

of cars in 2 sets.

$$\frac{1 \text{ set}}{8 \text{ cars}} = \frac{2 \text{ set}}{? \text{ cars}}$$

Refer to pages 6 through 20 in the Glossary for help.

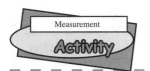

Word Bar

| Coin | Cost | Dime | Money | Nickel | Penny | Quarter |

Fill in the blanks with terms from the Word Bar.

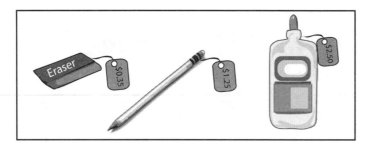

1. The _____ of the ✏️ 💲 is $1.25.

2. You can buy this pencil with _____.

3. You can buy the 🧽 with _____s, or metal pieces of money.

Circle the correct name for each coin.

4. 🪙   penny   nickel   dime   quarter

5. 🪙   penny   nickel   dime   quarter

6. 🪙   penny   nickel   dime   quarter

7. 🪙   penny   nickel   dime   quarter

Refer to pages 26 through 34 in the Glossary for help.

Time

Word Bar

Hour   Minute   Second

Label each picture with terms from the Word Bar.

1._____

2._____

Connect each term to the best phrase.

3. Hours   a. how long it takes to jump

4. Minutes   b. how long it takes to watch a movie

5. Seconds   c. how long it takes to count to 500

Refer to pages 28 through 34 in the Glossary for help.

Word Bar

Length	Foot	Inch	Mile	Ruler

Decide if each item should be measured in <u>inches</u>, <u>feet</u>, or <u>miles</u>.

1. the distance across your classroom   Inch   Foot   Mile

2. the length of your thumb   Inch   Foot   Mile

3. the distance from New York to Texas   Inch   Foot   Mile

4. the length of your pencil   Inch   Foot   Mile

Answer the questions using terms from the Word Bar.

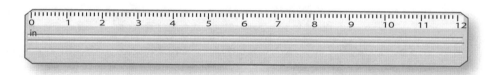

5. This tool is called a _____. It is used to measure _____,

or the distance of something.

Refer to pages 27 through 34 in the Glossary for help.

Mass

Word Bar

Mass	**Ounce**	**Pound**

How much matter does each of these items have? Circle your answer.

1.

    3 ounces   3 pounds

2.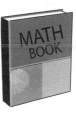

    2 ounces   2 pounds

3.

    25 ounces   25 pounds

4.

    1 ounce   1 pound

5. The _____ of something is the amount of matter it has.

Refer to pages 30 through 33 in the Glossary for help.

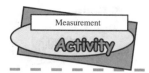

Measurement
Activity

Word Bar

| Capacity | Cup | Pint | Quart | Gallon |

How much can each item hold? Circle your answer.

1.

Cup   Quart

2.

Pint   Gallon

3.

Cup   Quart

4.

Pint   Gallon

5. The _____ of something is how much it can hold.

Refer to pages 26 through 34 in the Glossary for help.

Metric Measuring

Word Bar

Liter	Milliliter	Meter	Centimeter	Gram	Kilogram

Circle the term that is the best way to measure each item.

1. Length of your hand   Meter   Centimeter

2. Amount of water in a spoon   Liter   Milliliter

3. Weight of a cookie   Gram   Kilogram

4. Length of a truck   Meter   Centimeter

5. Weight of a dog   Gram   Kilogram

6. Amount of water in a pool   Liter   Milliliter

Refer to pages 26 through 31 in the Glossary for help.

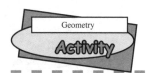

Word Bar

| Line | Line segment | Ray | Endpoint | Point | Plane |

Label each picture with a term from the Word Bar.

1._____

2._____

3._____

4._____

5._____

6._____

Lines

Word Bar

Parallel lines	**Perpendicular lines**	**Intersecting lines**	**Vertex**

Label each picture using a term from the Word Bar.

1._____

2._____

3._____

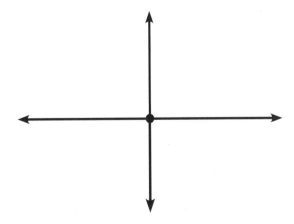

4._____

Refer to pages 40 through 54 in the Glossary for help.

Word Bar

| Straight angles | Supplementary angles | Protractor | Degrees |

Fill in the blanks using the terms from the Word Bar.

In math class, we learned about angles. There are many different kinds of angles. Angles that

measure 180° are called (1) _____. They look like this:

Angle A and Angle B together measure 180°. They are (2)_____.

I can measure these angles with a tool called a (3)_____. All angles are

measured in (4)_____.

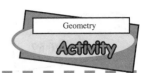

More Angles

Angle	Acute angle	Obtuse angle	Right angle

Answer the question using a term from the Word Bar.

1. When two line segments meet at one point, they create a(n) _____.

Look at the following angles. Circle if they are acute, right, or obtuse.

1.   Acute   Right   Obtuse

2.   Acute   Right   Obtuse

3.   Acute   Right   Obtuse

4.   Acute   Right   Obtuse

5.   Acute   Right   Obtuse

6.   Acute   Right   Obtuse

Refer to pages 35 through 49 in the Glossary for help.

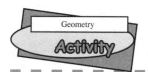
Word Bar

| Triangle | Acute triangle | Obtuse triangle | Right triangle |

Look at the following shapes.

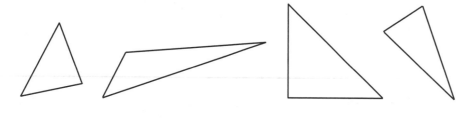

1. All of these shapes are called _____s.

Circle if each shape is an acute triangle, an obtuse triangle, or a right triangle.

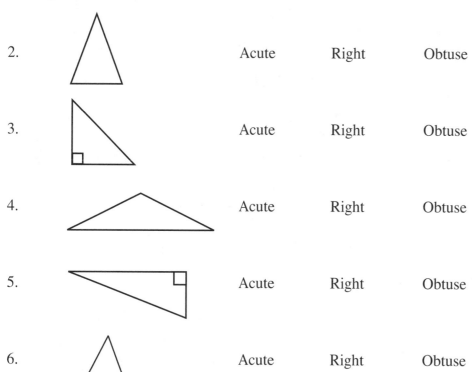

2.   Acute   Right   Obtuse

3.   Acute   Right   Obtuse

4.   Acute   Right   Obtuse

5.   Acute   Right   Obtuse

6.   Acute   Right   Obtuse

Refer to pages 35 through 53 in the Glossary for help.

© 2006 New Leaf Education

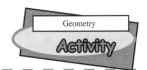

More Triangles

Word Bar

Equilateral triangle	Isosceles triangle	Scalene triangle
Congruent		

Connect the term on the left to its picture on the right.

1. Equilateral triangle   a.

2. Isosceles triangle   b.

3. Scalene triangle   c.

4. Draw a shape that is **congruent** to the shape provided.

Refer to pages 37 through 50 in the Glossary for help.

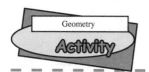

Word Bar

Square	Rectangle	Rhombus	Quadrilateral	Parallelogram
Trapezoid				

Circle the term that best describes each picture.

1.   Square   Trapezoid

2.   Rectangle   Rhombus

3.   Rhombus   Trapezoid

4.   Rhombus   Parallelogram

5.   Rectangle   Square

6. All of the figures above are _____ s.

Refer to pages 43 through 53 in the Glossary for help.

       © 2006 New Leaf Education

Polygons

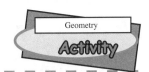

Word Bar

| Polygon | Regular polygon | Hexagon | Pentagon | Octagon |

Circle the term that best describes each picture.

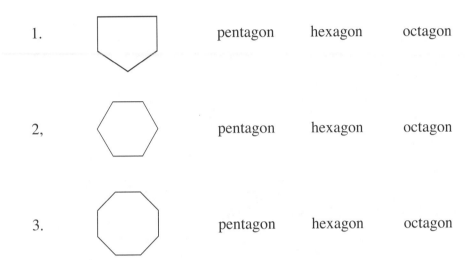

1.   pentagon   hexagon   octagon

2,   pentagon   hexagon   octagon

3.   pentagon   hexagon   octagon

Finish the sentences using terms from the Word Bar.

4. A shape made of straight lines is called a(n)_____.

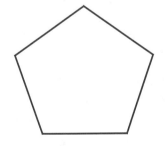

5. This shape is made of straight lines that have the same length.

It can be called a(n) _____.

Refer to pages 40 through 48 in the Glossary for help.

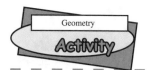

Word Bar

Circle	Diameter	Radius	Circumference
Center	Compass		

Label the pictures with terms from the Word Bar.

1._____

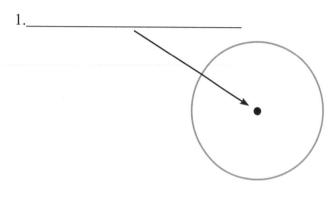

2._____   3._____

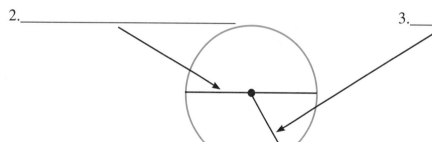

Finish the sentences with terms from the Word Bar.

4. The shapes shown above are called _____.

5. The distance around a circle is called the _____.

6. You can draw circles with a tool called a _____.

Refer to pages 36 through 46 in the Glossary for help.

3-D Shapes

Word Bar

| Cube | Pyramid | Rectangular prism | Triangular prism |

Circle the correct picture.

1. Cube

2. Rectangular prism

 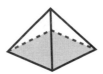 

3. Triangular prism

 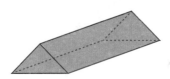

4. Pyramid

Refer to pages 38 through 53 in the Glossary for help.

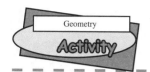

Word Bar

Cylinder   Sphere   Cone

Connect the picture on the right to the correct term on the left.

1. Cone

2. Cylinder

3. Sphere

Draw your own <u>cone</u>, <u>cylinder</u>, and <u>sphere</u> in the space provided.

Refer to pages 37 through 50 in the Glossary for help.

Parts of a Cube

Word Bar

Vertex   Base   Edge   Face   Net

Label the picture with terms from the Word Bar.

1._____

2._____

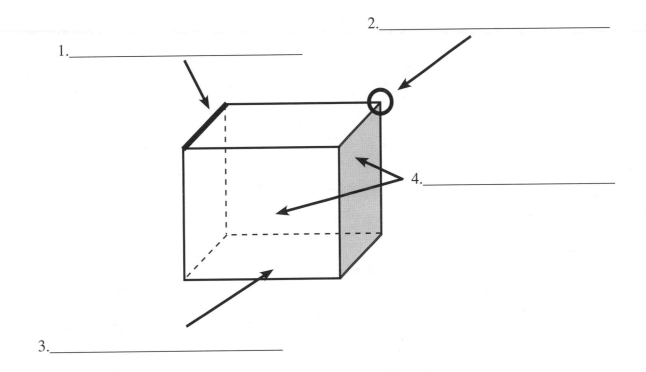

4._____

3._____

Look at the picture below.

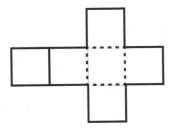

5. This picture can be folded to make a cube. It is an example of a(n) _____.

Refer to pages 36 through 54 in the Glossary for help.

Photocopying is illegal.

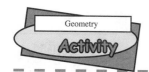

Word Bar

Perimeter	Area	Volume	Surface area	Tessellation

Fill in the blanks using terms from the Word Bar.

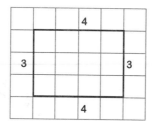

1. If you add the sides of this rectangle, you get 14. 14 is the _____.

2. If you multiply two sides of this rectangle, you get 12. 12 is the _____.

3. If you multiply the length, width, and height of this block, you get 4 × 3 × 2, or 24. 24 is the _____ of this block.

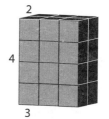

4. Find the surface area of this block_____.

5. The picture below shows shapes that connect together and cover the whole area. The picture is an example of _____.

Transformations

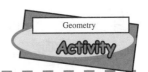
Word Bar

Reflect	Rotate	Translate	Symmetry
Line of symmetry	Transform		

Look at how each shape moves. Name the movement using terms from the Word Bar.

1.

   _____

2.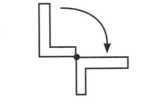

   _____

3.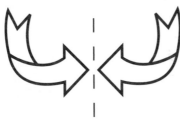

   _____

4. All of these movements are ways to _____ an object.

5. Circle the object that has **symmetry**. Draw a **line of symmetry** on the object.

Refer to pages 41 through 52 in the Glossary for help.

Word Bar

Data	Line plot	Table

Look at the examples and then answer the questions.

A.
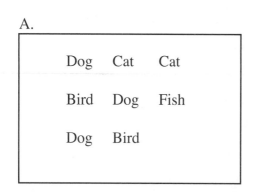

B.
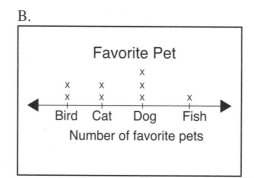

C.

Favorite Pet	Votes
Dog	3
Cat	2
Bird	2
Fish	1

1. **A** is an example of _____. It shows collected information.

2. **B** is an example of _____. It shows data using a number line.

3. **C** is an example of _____. It shows information in rows and columns.

Refer to pages 56 through 62 in the Glossary for help.

Graphs

Word Bar

Bar graph	Venn diagram	Tree diagram
Line graph	Circle graph	Pictograph
Stem-and-leaf plot		

Label each picture using terms from the Word Bar.

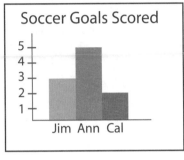

Soccer Goals Scored

1._____

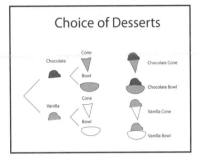

Choice of Desserts

2._____

Student Height (in inches)

Stem	Leaf
4	7 8
5	2 3 6
6	0

4 | 7 = 47 inches

3._____

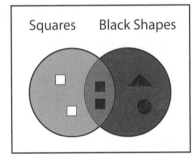

Squares   Black Shapes

4._____

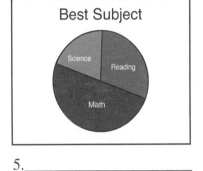

Best Subject

Science   Reading   Math

5._____

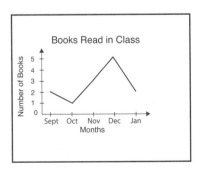

Books Read in Class

6._____

Money Earned

Mon Tues Wed Thurs

= 5 Dollars

7._____

Refer to pages 55 through 63 in the Glossary for help.

Photocopying is illegal.

Word Bar

| Mean | Median | Mode | Range | Outlier |

Fill in the blanks using terms from the Word Bar.

Game 1	Game 2	Game 3	Game 4	Game 5	Game 6
3	1	11	4	2	3

Danfield Baseball Team Scores

1. The _____ of the scores is 10. It is the difference between the greatest and least in the set.

2. The _____ of the scores is 11. This number is very different from the other numbers in the set.

3. The _____ of the scores is 4. It is the sum of all the scores divided by how many scores there are.

4. The _____ of the scores is 3. It is the middle number when the scores are written in order.

5. The _____ of the scores is 3. It is the number that occurs most often in the set.

Refer to pages 58 through 61 in the Glossary for help.

Population

Word Bar

Random sample	Bias sample	Population	Sample

For 1 and 2, one phrase describes a population. The other describes a sample of that population. Read and then check the correct box.

		Population	Sample
1.	the ages of students in your school	☐	☐
	the ages of students in the world	☐	☐
2.	all the red cars in your state	☐	☐
	all the red cars near your home	☐	☐

For 3 and 4, tell if you will get a random sample or a bias sample. Check the correct box.

	Random Sample	Bias Sample
3. What is your favorite animal?		
a) Ask students who own dogs.	☐	☐
b) Ask every fourth student in school.	☐	☐
4. What is your favorite subject in school?		
a) Ask math teachers.	☐	☐
b) Ask students in your class.	☐	☐

Refer to pages 55 through 61 in the Glossary for help.

Word Bar

Certain	Equally likely	Impossible	Most likely
Probability	Least likely	Outcome	

There are seven shapes in the bag. You pick one without looking. Circle the term that best answers the questions below.

1. It is (**most likely** , **least likely**) that you will pick a square.

2. It is (**equally likely** , **least likely**) that you will pick either a triangle or a circle.

3. It is (**certain** , **least likely**) that you will pick a shape.

4. It is (**most likely** , **impossible**) that you will pick a white shape.

5. The (**outcome** , **probability**) that you will pick a square is 1/7.

6. It is (**certain** , **impossible**) that you will pick a red shape.

7. There are seven possible (**outcomes** , **probabilities**) of picking a shape.

Refer to pages 55 through 60 in the Glossary for help.

Algebra (1)

Word Bar

Pattern   Function table

Look at the table. Then answer the questions using terms from the Word Bar.

T-Shirt	Cost
1	$10
2	$20
3	$30

1. This is an example of a _____.

2. How much would the cost be for four t-shirts? _____

3. 10, 20, 30... is an example of a _____. The numbers follow a rule.

Refer to pages 65 through 66 in the Glossary for help.

Word Bar

Coordinate plane	X-axis	Y-axis	Ordered pair

Look at the diagram. Fill in the blanks using terms from the Word Bar.

1. _____

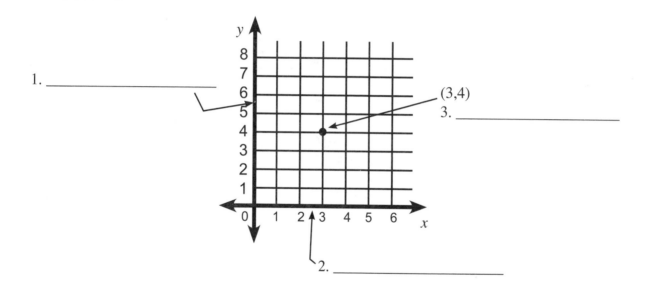

(3,4)

3. _____

2. _____

4. The diagram above is known as a(n) _____.

Refer to pages 64 through 67 in the Glossary for help.

Word Bar

Algebraic expression	Equation	Order of operations	Variable

Answer the questions with the terms from the Word Bar.

1. *b* + 6   This can be called a(n) _____.

2. *b* + 6 = 8   This can be called a(n) _____.

3. In the group *c* − 3 = 5, the letter *c* is called a(n) _____.

Gita is doing her math homework. Here is her problem:	**9 + (6 − 4) × 5**
First, Gita computes all the numbers in the parentheses.	9 + (2) × 5
Next, Gita multiplies from left to right.	9 + 10
Last, Gita adds from left to right.	19

4. Gita has used the _____ to help her figure out the problem.

Refer to pages 64 through 66 in the Glossary for help.

Notes

Notes